Startup Strategy

The Art of The Start for Solopreneurs, Even if You Already Started

Ric Thompson

Ric Thompson

Just to say Thank You for Purchasing this Book I want to give you a gift <u>100% absolutely FREE</u>

A Copy of My Special Report "*Outsource Time*"

Go to
www.DoneForYouSolutions.com/OutsourceTime
to Receive Your FREE Gift

Startup Strategy

© 2014

All Rights Reserved. No part of this publication may be reproduced in any form or by any means, including scanning, photocopying, or otherwise without prior written permission of the copyright holder.

Disclaimer and Terms of Use: The Author and Publisher have strived to be as accurate and complete as possible in the creation of this book, notwithstanding the fact that they do not warrant or represent at any time that the contents within are accurate due to the rapidly changing nature of the Internet. While all attempts have been made to verify information provided in this publication, the Author and Publisher assume no responsibility for errors, omissions, or contrary interpretation of the subject matter herein. Any perceived slights of specific persons, peoples, or organizations are unintentional. In practical advice books, like anything else in life, there are no guarantees of income made or health benefits received. This book is not intended for use as a source of medical, legal, business, accounting or financial advice. All readers are advised to seek services of competent professionals in medical, legal, business, accounting, and finance matters.

Printed in the United States of America

Table of Contents

INTRODUCTION	6
WHAT IS A BUSINESS STRATEGY?	7
WHAT'S YOUR STRATEGY SCORE?	9
SECTION #1: WORK "ON" YOUR BUSINESS NOT "IN" IT	12
DEFINING YOUR ROLE IN YOUR BUSINESS	13
The Technician	*14*
The Manager	*14*
The Entrepreneur	*14*
WEARING THE CEO HAT	15
BUSINESS GOALS	16
Defining Your Goals	*16*
BUSINESS EXPECTATIONS	17
TOOLS OF THE CEO TRADE	18
SWOT Analysis	*19*
Working Business Plan	*20*
WHEN SHOULD YOU WEAR THE CEO HAT?	21
WHAT'S YOUR BUSINESS STRATEGY?	22
SECTION #2: BUSINESS MODELS AND COMPETITIVE ADVANTAGE	24
HOW DO YOU INTEND TO MAKE MONEY?	24
OPTIMIZING THE CLIENT EXPERIENCE	27
Defining Your Funnel	*28*
Mapping your Model	*29*
IDENTIFYING YOUR COMPETITIVE ADVANTAGE	29
DEFINING YOUR USP	30
GET TO KNOW YOUR COMPETITION	31
IDENTIFYING YOUR CUSTOMER	33
PLAN TO SUCCEED	34
SECTION #3: DEAL MAKING AND NEGOTIATION	35
WHAT IS DEAL MAKING AND NEGOTIATION?	35
KNOW WHEN TO NEGOTIATE	36
HOW TO NEGOTIATE SUCCESSFULLY	37
HOW TO BE COMFORTABLE NEGOTIATING	38
HOW TO IMPROVE YOUR NEGOTIATION SKILLS	39
PREPARING FOR A NEGOTIATION	40
PRACTICE NEGOTIATING	41

SECTION #4: FUNDING AND GETTING YOUR BUSINESS UP AND RUNNING — 42

    FINANCING YOUR BUSINESS, YOUR FIRST STEP — 42
    WHAT ARE YOUR FINANCING OPTIONS? — 44
    WHAT DO YOU NEED FOR A SMALL BUSINESS LOAN? — 45
    DEVELOPING YOUR BUSINESS PLAN — 46
        Common Components of a Business Plan — 47
    SELF-FUNDING — 50
    CAN YOU AFFORD TO START YOUR BUSINESS? — 50

INSPIRED ACTION — 54

WHAT'S YOUR STRATEGY SCORE NOW? — 56

CONCLUSION — 59

CHECK OUT SOME OF RIC'S OTHER BOOKS!! — 61

Introduction

I want to thank you and congratulate you for purchasing *"**Startup Strategy, The Art of The Start for Solopreneurs, Even if You Already Started."***

This book provides everything you need to understand the importance of developing a business strategy and how you can use that strategy to start and manage your business successfully.

After reading this guide, you will understand the basic components of a business strategy, how to set business goals, and the tools you can use to help you build your business. You will understand the difference between business expectations and business goals, and the importance of measuring success for both of them.

 If you are ready to build the business of your dreams and seek out the success you know you can achieve, starting with a sound strategy is the first step on the way to making that goal a reality. From learning how to produce a SWOT Analysis to walking you through the first draft of your business plan, this guide gives you immediately applicable information that you can use today to make a difference in your business and your life.

With the help of Startup Strategy, you're on your way to achieving just about anything you can imagine. Thanks again for purchasing, I hope you enjoy it!

Ric Thompson

What is a Business Strategy?

Running your own business takes a desire to succeed. It takes having a dream. It also takes much more than that. While it would be nice to simply have a dream and have it come true, running your own business successfully takes having a business strategy.

While still in high school, Bill Gates had a passion for writing code and programming computers. He also had a dream. He wanted to see programmers receive compensation for their skills. He wanted them to be able to charge for their work and efforts. Microsoft didn't come into existence simply because Gates had a dream. He also had a strategy.

Bill Gates wrote a letter in 1976 to hobby programmers saying that MITS, the company he'd partnered with, could not continue to produce, distribute, and maintain high-quality software without payment. It was the first step of his strategy which led to the foundation of today's Microsoft, their mission statement, and their success. Today, Microsoft is still described as a "developer centric" business. Developers and programmers are highly recruited and highly compensated.

His strategy was obviously a success.

What does it take to start and run a successful business? Strategy!

A business strategy encompasses a myriad of topics, including everything from how you form your company, whether you are a sole proprietorship or a corporation, to how you charge your customers, and even how you position yourself in your market.

Your business strategy is how, why, where, and with whom you do business. How you deliver your product or service and even how you assess your business. For example, do you review your profits and losses each month, quarter, or at the end of the year? Your business plan addresses how you obtain financing, whom you partner with and how, and who operates your business and handles tasks.

A business strategy begins with an idea ...

...and ends with your exit strategy. Your exit strategy isn't as simple as selling your company, although it can be. You can put your company on the public market – an IPO. You can negotiate an acquisition, you can liquidate it, and you can shut it down. Strategy is your business from start to finish. How it's going to get up and running, how it's going to be successful, and how you're going to exit the business when you're done. Your business strategy is your road map to success. To be a good map, it has to be comprehensive and all-encompassing. Without a comprehensive business strategy, you will be operating in the dark.

Startup Strategy

What's Your Strategy Score?

A sound strategy is crucial for your business success. You know the saying, "If you don't know where you're going, you'll never know when you get there"? The strategy is not only the destination, but the map for how to get there and the method of transportation you're going to use. It's as simple as that.

Before we get started, spend a few minutes and take this evaluation based on how strategic your business is today. You'll retake it again after reading the guide to see where you've made progress. It's a great tool to evaluate what you've learned.

On a scale of 1-10 (10 being the highest), rank where you currently stand with regard to your business strategy.

I understand the roles of the Technician, the Manager, and the Entrepreneur, and how they apply to my business.

1   2   3   4   5   6   7   8   9   10

I have written long and short term goals as well as a 5-10 year vision for my business.

1   2   3   4   5   6   7   8   9   10

I have a clear picture of my, and my business', Strengths and the competitive advantage that gives us.

1   2   3   4   5   6   7   8   9   10

Ric Thompson

I have a clear picture of my weaknesses and those of my business, and how to compensate for that.

1   2   3   4   5   6   7   8   9   10

I have a clear picture of my opportunities and those of my business and how to capitalize on them.

1   2   3   4   5   6   7   8   9   10

I have a clear picture of the possible threats to me and my business and how to minimize them.

1   2   3   4   5   6   7   8   9   10

I have a defined business model and a structure for how my clients will go through it.

1   2   3   4   5   6   7   8   9   10

I know how my top three competitors do business and how I am differentiating myself.

1   2   3   4   5   6   7   8   9   10

I know exactly who my clients are and what they want

1   2   3   4   5   6   7   8   9   10

Startup Strategy

I understand the process of a negotiation and all the questions I need to know the answers to before I go into a negotiation

1   2   3   4   5   6   7   8   9   10

I have a good understanding of the funding sources available to my business for start-up or expansion

SCORING

Add up all the numbers you circled._____

Divide the total number by 10

Record your "Strategy Score" here _____

Section #1: Work "ON" your Business Not "IN" It

> *"The person who figures out how to harness the collective genius of his or her organization is going to blow the competition away."*
> - *Walter Wriston*

When you own your own business you wear many hats. Own a coaching business and you're the coach, you're the marketing executive, you're the sales staff, you're the administrative assistant, you're the bookkeeper, copywriter, and maybe even the accountant. You may be the web designer, the help desk, and so much more. Owning and operating a business means you're all of those people. It is one of the joys of owning a business for some and a dilemma for others.

Consider, for a moment the owner of a restaurant. As the owner, you're probably at your restaurant most nights that it's open. When you're there, you're opening doors for your customers. You're wandering the floor of the restaurant making sure everyone is happy. You're probably also in the kitchen making sure everything is running smoothly. And if your restaurant is like many, you're solving problems left and right. This customer needs something. This waitperson needs something else. The kitchen is out of tomatoes and so on.

When the restaurant isn't open, you're probably ordering supplies. Maybe going over profits and expenses. You might be hiring staff to help run your restaurant. You might be meeting with specialists like graphic designers for your menu or your signage or an accountant. You might be in the kitchen working on new menu items or helping your bartender stock the bar.

Startup Strategy

If you're running your restaurant 24/7, when do you have time to sit back and look at what you need to do to build your business? When do you have time to consider franchising? When do you look at how your competition is doing and how you can differentiate yourself?

That is the challenge many business owners face – setting aside time to analyze their business. Setting aside time to work on their business rather than in it.

Owning a business, any business, whether it is brick and mortar, an online business, or a combination of both, means you're responsible for wearing a variety of hats. Among them is the CEO hat.

Being the CEO means you're in charge of how your business grows, how your business positions itself against your competition, how your business is funded, your business model and your business strategy.

Right here, right now you're going to put on your CEO hat …

Ready? Is it on?

Let's make sure. Let's define the other hats you could be wearing at any particular moment.

Defining Your Role in Your Business

Michael Gerber, world-renowned small business expert and author of the bestselling books *The E-Myth* and *The E-Myth Revisited*, defines three roles a business owner plays at any particular time. They are:

The Technician

You're probably most familiar with the role of the Technician. The majority of people who start a business begin as a technician. For example, a website designer may have started their career as a graphic designer. They graduated from college and went into the workforce. They spent five, 10, or maybe even 25 years working for someone else. Then they got the bug, the bug to be their own boss and own their own business.

Why not? They understand website and graphic design inside and out. Who better to own a website design business?

The technician is the doer of a business. They are vital to the success of the business, as is each role. The Technician is the person who gets things done. The Technician, using the website designer example, sits down and designs websites. They get busy performing the core work customers are paying for.

The Manager

The next role is that of the Manager. The Manager is the planner. The Manager is the person that keeps structure and order to the business. The Manager creates systems that help the operation flow smoothly. The Manager recognizes problems and develops a structure to resolve the problems.

The Entrepreneur

The last role and the role that is important for the remainder of the lesson is that of the Entrepreneur. The Entrepreneur is a role that often gets pushed into the corner once the business is up and running. The Entrepreneur is the creative, innovative, risk-taking side of us. The Entrepreneur sees opportunity around every corner. The Entrepreneur is excited about the future and has big dreams for the business.

So, now ask yourself this question -

What's your role in your business?

Take a few minutes to think about what role you most frequently play in your business. Are you most often the Technician? The Manager? The Entrepreneur? There's no right or wrong answer here. The purpose of pondering this question is to help you realize where you spend the majority of your time so you can recognize it and strive to find a balance between all three roles.

Wearing the CEO Hat

Working on your business rather than in it, is the role of the Entrepreneur, the CEO. When you're wearing this hat, which you are right now, right? When you wear this hat, you recognize that your business is separate from your life. Your business is something that is separate from you.

When you're working on your business rather than in it, you're asking yourself these kinds of questions:

- How can I own my business and have a life apart from it?
- How can I spend my time doing the work that I love (rather than the work you think you have to do)?

We look at the answers to these questions in more depth in "***Being an Entrepreneur: The Solopreneur's Guide to Living the Dream Without Losing it!***" where we also cover time management, effective use of time, personal development, and creating a life outside of your business.

Here we're going to focus how to stand apart from your business as the CEO and take a critical look at how it is performing and how it can improve.

Business Goals

When Bill Gates started Microsoft, he had the goal of making sure programmers and developers were rewarded financially for their efforts. To this day, that goal is being met ten-fold. Microsoft developers are among the highest paid in the industry.

A business goal is a statement that defines where you want to take your business. It can be a micro goal such as "I want to sell 100 widgets this month," or it can be a macro goal like "I want to be known for having the best customer service in the industry." Chances are your business will have many goals. By understanding where you want to go with your business, it helps you build a better strategy to achieve it – a strategy that puts you at the helm and places the right people in your business to help you reach your goals.

Defining Your Goals

Let's begin by examining the goals you have for your business.

Grab a notebook that you can use to record thoughts, ideas, and actions as your move through this guide. Label the first page 'GOALS' and answer the following questions.

What are your long-term and short-term business goals?

Startup Strategy

What will your business look like in five to 10 years?

How are you going to achieve these goals? For example, if you said you wanted to increase your customer list by 10% by the end of the year, how are you going to do it?

What is your strategy?

How are you going to measure your success?

When will you determine if you've met your goals?

How will you assess them?

> *"However beautiful the strategy, you should occasionally look at the results."*
> -*Winston Churchill*

Business Expectations

To expect something is to look forward to it. A synonym for expect is hope.

- What do your customers expect when they do business with you?
- What does your staff expect?
- What do you expect?

What do you expect, not what are your goals. Goals are different from expectations. Goals are smaller plans for your business. Some example for these might be sales goals, time commitment goals, and staffing goals.

Expectations are different from goals. As a business owner you design your business to meet the needs and expectations of your customers, your staff, and you. We're talking about expectations here, not needs. A customer can visit your website because they need to buy a health supplement. However, they expect to find a well laid-out website. They expect good customer service. They expect secure purchasing.

Turn to a new page in your notebook, and capture your responses to the following questions to help you determine if your business is currently meeting expectations.

Is your business meeting expectations?

How is your business meeting the expectations of your customers?

How is your business meeting the expectations of employees?

How is your business meeting your expectations?

What expectations is your business not meeting?

How can your business exceed the expectations of your customers? Be creative here and think out of the box. Surprise your customers by meeting expectations they didn't know they had.

Tools of the CEO Trade

We've spent a bit of time wearing the CEO hat. How are you feeling? Sometimes, particularly when you're used to wearing the technician or manager hat, being the CEO feels a bit overwhelming. If you're feeling besieged, now is the time to take a break. The next segment of this lesson will delve into some serious analytical tools and questions. It's important to have a clear mind and to be feeling like an Entrepreneur – excited and passionate about the future.

Startup Strategy

In your technician and manager roles, it is very likely that you have tools of the trade that you use to work in your business and to manage aspects of your business. The CEO part of your role also has tools, and you need to learn how and when to use them in order to be as effective as possible when you are wearing your CEO hat.

Putting on the CEO hat begins with a careful, consistent, and continuous evaluation of your business. Let's begin with...

SWOT Analysis

SWOT stands for Strengths, Weaknesses, Opportunities, and Threats. It is an extremely helpful tool that enables you to step outside of your business and take a critical look at it. SWOT helps you examine where you can improve your business and where you're already very strong.

This analysis will help you position yourself against your competition in a manner that makes the most sense. For example, if you want to beat your competition by offering the absolute best customer service, but your current customer service strategy is weak, or you don't have the technology to support it, then you know how to plan. You can either improve your technology or you can find a different way to position your company against your competition.

A SWOT analysis gives you the information you need to make good decisions about where to focus your energies, who to hire, and what tasks are important. You're the entrepreneur, the captain of your ship. It is your job to drive the business, and your SWOT will guide you to that end.

To perform a SWOT analysis, label a new page in your notebook "SWOT Analysis," and add today's date to the page. Then start by listing out all of the strengths of the business. This includes things that make you special, better, or different than other businesses and competitors.

Next, write out all of the businesses weaknesses. This includes things that people don't like or have commented as not being exemplary. Ask yourself where you feel the business is falling down or where it needs to be stronger.

After that, switch gears a little and start recording all the current opportunities you can think of including new products, new services, expanded offerings, and better customer service.

Lastly, write down the threats the company is facing. What is holding it back and threatening the overall success of the business? What could keep it from achieving the objectives?

Working Business Plan

It is vital to your business' success to create a "working business plan." A working business plan is a business plan which is revisited on a regular basis and modified or changed as your business goals, strategies, and business model change. If your business plan is set in stone, it doesn't leave any room for flexibility, to take advantage of opportunities, to resolve issues, or to change with the times.

For example, what would you do if a national hardware chain opened up right next to your local hardware store?

This happened to the owner of a small hardware store. After a period of panic and confusion, the storeowner placed a sign on the front of his store that said, "Main Entrance." This strategy pulled his store out of the shadows and brought customers right into his store.

Startup Strategy

He put on his CEO hat and found a strategy that worked. I wonder what would have happened had he been wearing his CEO hat more frequently. Possibly he might have had a strategy in place BEFORE the national chain moved in and wouldn't have suffered those months of lost sales and confusion.

To have a working business plan, it means occasionally putting on that CEO hat. It means possibly stepping out of the roles you're more comfortable in, the technician or the manager, and stepping out of your business. It means working on your business rather than in it.

When Should You Wear the CEO Hat?

Take a look at your schedule, and plan when you're going to put your CEO hat on. Identify specific times when you will commit to working on your business rather than in it. Ask yourself how often you are going to review and evaluate your business. You might decide you need this kind of review weekly, monthly, or even quarterly. Regardless of the frequency you choose, you need to plan and schedule when you're going to work on your business rather than work in it to ensure it happens.

Now that you have committed to a specific time, think about what needs to happen to make sure you can dedicate that time to wearing your CEO hat. What do you need to do to make that happen? For example, do you need to set aside the first Monday of the month, block appointments, or phone calls? Do you need to hire or outsource to make the time? Do you need to join a mastermind group that meets regularly to help inspire and stimulate your entrepreneurial mind?

Make a list in your notebook of the actions you need to take to make sure you can keep this commitment, and then make sure you take care of those things before your scheduled time arrives.

What's Your Business Strategy?

The later sections of this guide delve into the specifics of your business, from choosing your business model to negotiation skills, which means for the rest of this guide you'll be wearing your CEO hat. To set the foundation for the rest of that work, you need to evaluate your current business strategy.

Write "STRATEGY" at the top of a page in your notebook, and then answer these questions from the position of how things are done in your business RIGHT NOW. If you haven't started your business yet, write down how you THINK things will be.

What is your business? Define it.

Who are your customers and what do they need/want? (Age, demographics)

How do you reach your customers? Via internet, bricks and mortar location, the mail, phone or fax, making house calls?

Do you reach them with some combination of communication methods?

How do you advertise and market to your customers?

How do you differentiate yourself from your competition?

What strengths do you have that make you and your business standout?

Startup Strategy

What weaknesses do you have, and how can you overcome them? For example, low startup financing may be a weakness, and a small business loan may be your solution.

How do you charge your customers?

Why are you in business?

What are your goals?

What is your exit strategy?

How and when do you plan to eventually leave the business?

Section #2: Business Models and Competitive Advantage

The latest statistics published by the Small Business Administration (SBA) tell us that "two-thirds of new employer establishments survive at least two years, and 44% survive at least four years."

What do these numbers say? They demonstrate that it is getting easier to succeed in business. Previous statistics demonstrated that only about 5% of new businesses made it to four years. That just isn't the case anymore.

One of the reasons why businesses are more capable of succeeding may be the easy access to information and guides like this one that help new business owners stay in business. Another reason may be that entrepreneurs are recognizing the importance of having a business strategy. They know the importance of having a proper business model and of positioning themselves correctly with their competition.

While more businesses are succeeding than ever before, if you look carefully at the statistics, you'll see that less than half of new business owners go the distance and last longer than four years. What can you do to make sure your business survives?

It all begins with your business model. There are tons of different models that could work for your business and there is no right or wrong model. Let's begin by taking a look at how to choose the optimal business model for your particular business.

How Do You Intend to Make Money?

That is the essential question you must ask yourself to begin determining which business model is right for you. Your business model is how you make money. Are you a service-based business that charges by the hour or a product-based business that sells directly to the consumer? Do you combine the two?

If you're a service-based business, you might answer this question by stating that you're going to charge $100 an hour for your services. Great! If you're billing 20 hours a week then you're going to make a nice salary - $100,000.

However, with this business model, you also want to plan how you're going to obtain your customers. It may be that it takes more than 20 hours a week to generate those 20 billable hours. So now you're working 40 hours a week plus to generate customers and billable hours. During the time you're working to obtain and generate customers, you're not making any money. This means your non-billable hours bring your hourly value down to $50 an hour, which is $100,000/40 hours a week. To increase your hourly value, you may want to adjust your business model.

To solve your problem, you could raise your hourly rates to $125 an hour. Now your hourly value has increased, however, it may be more difficult to find clients who are willing to pay $125 an hour for your services. So you see, there's more to a business plan than simply how much you're going to charge. You also have to determine what tasks go into making a profit.

If you're a service-based business, you might have one of the following business models:

Charge by the day or half-day – This model means you require a minimum from your clients. This helps you avoid short appointments and it means fewer clients to meet the same hourly profits. This also means less time spent on obtaining new clients.

What types of businesses could benefit from this type of model? Massage therapists, personal or professional coaches, fitness coaches, and professional organizers could all benefit from this model.

Charge by the project or charge a flat fee – This model gives you time to plan and schedule. It also makes it easier for you to predict your cash flow, particularly if your projects are generally long-term projects. This model also makes it possible for you to bill for your research and admin time which results in a higher hourly value.

What types of businesses could profit from this model? Writers, designers, programmers, and virtual assistants could benefit most from this model.

Charge a monthly retainer – This business model makes it easy for you to charge clients by the month in advance, which means you can also charge for your availability. Your retainer guarantees you a fixed number of hours, which means that you can spend more time creating new business. Marketing and creating business is an absolute necessity for the success of any business or business model. It's so important that we've developed an entire guide dedicated to marketing your business.

A virtual assistant is a great example of someone who can utilize this type of business model successfully. Additionally, a coach, nutritionist, or housekeeper could also take advantage of this model.

Take the core of what you love, do that, and outsource the rest. We'll talk more about outsourcing later – just remember as we go that you don't have to do it all alone.

If you're a product-based business, meaning you sell a product, whether it is information or a tangible product like a

Startup Strategy

Frisbee or a lawn chair, you might have one of the following business models.

Charge a standard or flat fee – This is the most common type of product business model. You can offer a wide variety of products each at a different price.

Charge a subscription or membership fee – Many product-based businesses operate with a subscription model. For example, you can sell a membership to your gym. Information products are also often offered on a subscription basis.

You can also use a combination of pricing or business models to meet both the needs of your clients, to optimize your time, and make the most profits.

Now looking at these basic "models" is where most business people stop, and they end up struggling in their business because of it.

The model isn't just about how you get paid; it's about the client experience, why they stay with your business, and the value that is exchanged between you.

Optimizing the Client Experience

To make the most of this relationship between you and your customer, to create a client experience, it is often helpful to create a product line or what's known as a "product funnel." A product funnel is defined as a product line where the price of the product gradually progresses upward. Imagine the widest part of the funnel the point where your clients enter. The point of your funnel is your highest priced product. The goal is to sell your clients as many products in your funnel as make sense for them to buy.

The concept works like this:

Step #1: You convert a prospect into a client by selling him a product. It can be any level of product in your funnel.

Step #2: Upsell your client by convincing them to buy the next highest-priced item in your funnel. This is also called a back-end sale. An example is when you go to McDonalds to buy a burger, and they ask you if you want fries with that. The fries are the back-end sale. If you don't include this concept of back-end sales into your business model, you're leaving money on the table, and you're not giving your customers the experience they desire. Who wants to eat a burger without fries?!

Step #3: Continue to offer them the other items in your funnel. The pattern continues until your client chooses to no longer buy from you.

Defining Your Funnel

Having a product line and offering multiple price levels ensures that each and every client goes away happy. It also ensures that you are making the maximum amount of profits from each client. Think about your clients for a moment, how can you help them better meet their needs with a product funnel?

For example, if you have a sick pet, are you more likely to buy just one book on pet illness, or would you buy several on different types of illness, and maybe some vitamins or supplements for the pet? Get the picture?

What is the purpose of your business on a macro level? What is the experience of the client supposed to be? Once you know that your business model, including your business

Startup Strategy

funnel, is the map, it will enable you to give your client the experience you intend them to have.

Mapping your Model

Grab your notebook and use the following questions to create a map of your business model.

- How will customers find out about your business?
- What is the next logical step for them to take in the process?
- What is step 2?
- How about step 3? And so on...

Don't worry if all of these steps aren't in place or built just yet, just get the concept for now. We'll go into more detail for how to get this stuff done in the Marketing guide.

Your model will often be your competitive advantage, but let's take a deeper look

Identifying Your Competitive Advantage

One way to determine the optimal model and plan for your business is to take a look at what your competition is doing. How are they making money, and how can you learn from them while differentiating yourself from them? How can you position your business in a light that is more appealing to potential clients?

When determining your competitive advantage, grab your notebook, and record your answers to the following questions:

- What can your company do better than any other company?
- Can you offer better service?

- Faster delivery?
- A more powerful product?
- What can you do better than your competition, and does that really matter?
- Why does the business exist, and what is its purpose?
- What is your mission statement, and what have you promised to yourself and your customers? For example, Kraft Foods has the following mission statement: "Helping People Around the World Eat and Live Better"

It doesn't have to be everything. One simple promise that you always follow through on can be the key to success.

EXAMPLE 1 – McDonald's hamburgers are consistent, fast, and cheap regardless of where in the world you buy one. They aren't a GOOD hamburger. They don't have a lot of toppings or options. Their competitive advantage isn't the hamburger at all, it's the system.

EXAMPLE 2 – Zappos.com, an online shoe store, has free shipping and free returns. Their prices in general are not cheaper than any other online shoe store. However, the ability to return your shoes for free is a huge draw for many customers. It is the one thing they do better than any other online shoe store. They make it as easy as printing out a form, taping it on the box, and dropping it off at the post office.

Defining Your USP

Your Unique Selling Proposition or USP tells your prospects why they should do business with YOU. It is generally stated as a slogan. For example, M&Ms has one of the most memorable ones ever. Do you remember it? "M&Ms. Melts in your mouth, not in your hands." That makes them unique from all other chocolate candies. It differentiates them, makes them stand out, and tells the client exactly what they'll get. Another example is from Domino's Pizza. "Fresh Hot Pizza in 30 Minutes or Less – Guaranteed." The slogan is memorable because it is short and to the point.

Your USP tells customers and clients what makes you better, special, and different from all of the other people in the world out there trying to sell them your product or service. It also tells them why they need to work with you rather than continuing to do what they're doing, or not doing anything at all.

Your USP needs to be specific, concise, and most importantly, make an emotional connection with your target prospect. The USP is crucial. Without it your sales team has no focus, nothing with which to tempt their prospects. Realize that you can have more than one USP. The idea is not to sum up your entire business in one sentence.

To help you define your USP, answer the following questions in your notebook.

- What makes you unique?
- Why is your service the only one they should consider?
- Why should they even bother with your product or service in the first place?

Get to Know Your Competition

Who is your competition? A pizza company entering the Denver market for the first time ran a promotion offering two pizzas for the price of one if customers tore out and brought in their competitions yellow pages ad. They knew their competition and developed a sneaky strategy to put themselves in the forefront of customer's minds. You can't call the competition if you don't have their phone number!

It all begins with research. Researching your competition is the first step to developing a competitive advantage. Find out as much about your competition as you can. This will likely involve:

- Visiting their website
- Searching publications for articles, references, and press releases
- Reading about the company founders
- Reading their financial statements, if they're available
- Learning their mission statement
- Assessing how they do business. Do they have any weaknesses or flaws? You can often find this information by visiting relevant forums online. For example, if the business sells kitchen appliances, you can visit their blog or forum if they have one to read complaints about the company, or you can visit relevant forums or blogs and search for posts related to the company.
- Looking at their advertising and seeing what works and what doesn't. You can usually bet that if you see an ad being run repeatedly it works. Study it and find out how they are appealing to YOUR potential clients.

Once you know more about your competitors, you can identify where you are different and how to turn those differences into competitive advantages.

Startup Strategy

Identifying Your Customer

Who is your customer? Researching your customer is another step toward developing a competitive advantage. You need to understand what needs or wants your customer has that aren't being fulfilled, or which things are being fulfilled well, by your competition? Customer research is handled a number or ways. Forums and chat rooms on your business website are a great way to learn what your customer needs.

Additionally, other forums and chat rooms are also a significant tool. If you sell shoes online and you want to know what your customer needs, visit other shopping sites and read their forums.

Surveys are another helpful tool. Simply ask your clients and customers what they want. Surveys can be posted on your website, emailed, or mailed out to your current customers. For simple online solutions, check out SurveyMonkey.com and AskDatabase.com

You need to gather enough information so that you can record the following in your notebook. Be as thorough and detailed as possible.

- Describe your ideal client in detail.
- What are their demographics?
- Why do they use your product or service?
- What are they looking for?
- What solutions do they need?
- How much are they willing to spend?
- Is that purchase an easy decision or is it difficult?

Plan to Succeed

Once you know who your competition is, what differentiates you from them, and who your customers are and what they need, you have the information you need to build out your business strategy based on your competitive advantages.

Develop your strategy and figure out how to incorporate your competitive advantage into your daily business activities, and then take action. Research is a futile effort unless you use it to take action.

> **"There is no elevator to success. You have to take the stairs."**
> *-Anonymous*

Startup Strategy

Section #3: Deal Making and Negotiation

What is Deal Making and Negotiation?

Negotiation, or the fine art of getting what you want from another person who may or may not want to give it to you, is an intimidating practice for many. Most of us can relate to the experience of buying a new car. The thought of going into the car dealership to buy a car makes many shake. You know that there is a marked price on the car, and you know how much you can afford or want to pay. What you don't know is how low the dealer will go, and if they'll be willing to meet your needs. Hence, most people think car salesmen use the fear and intimidation factor. However, if you want to walk away with a car and most of your money, you need to learn how to negotiate with confidence. Likewise, if you want to have a successful business, negotiating skills are critical to the lasting success of your business.

Here is what negotiation isn't:

Negotiation isn't winning at someone else's expense. Negotiation is finding a win-win solution. Both you and the person you're working with will walk away from the table with a satisfying solution.

Negotiation isn't aggressive. It isn't passive either. Negotiation is like defensive driving. You want to make sure you're prepared for anything that comes up, and you want all the cars on the road to make it home safely.

> *"In business, you don't get what you deserve, you get what you negotiate."*
> -*Chester L. Karrass*

Negotiation isn't talking until you get your way. Negotiation is a skill of listening, hearing what your partner wants or needs, and then making it happen in a manner that is mutually beneficial.

Know When to Negotiate

Just about every task in business requires some sort of negotiation.

For example, if you're hiring a new employee or outsourcing a project, your negotiation might include salary and benefits. It may also include how often the person is paid, how long it will take to complete a task, and how you will communicate during the project.

When you're working with a vendor, you'll also need to negotiate. Possibilities include price, delivery date, and delivery time.

Joint Venture Partnerships also require a heady amount of negotiation. Joint ventures can range from swapping advertising space in your company e-zine to partnering to create a new product. Who handles what, how the tasks are accounted for including checks and balances, and how the profits are divided and paid are all points to be negotiated.

Client relations may also require negotiation skills. For example, if you have a customer that wants to return an item that is clearly beyond your stated policy, you will likely want to find a solution that makes your customer happy and doesn't cost your business too much.

Funding and investors are also a potential negotiation point. While many lenders and investors have strict terms, 10% APR and 36 month payment terms, others will allow some sort of negotiation, particularly if you have something to offer. When you negotiate for a new car, often you can get the price of the car to drop if you have money to put up front. The same holds true for some business loans. The larger collateral you provide the smaller interest rate you have to pay.

So now you know when you might have to negotiate, how to do successfully it is another matter.

> *"The most important trip you may take in life is meeting people half way."*
> *- Henry Boyle*

How to Negotiate Successfully

The first step to successful negotiation is to be comfortable with the concept. If you're anxious, nervous, combative, or defensive during the negotiations, they're not likely to go very well at all. Imagine sitting down with someone who has their arms crossed and a frown on their face. Even if they have something you really want or need for your business, you're not likely to want to do business with them.

Once you're truly comfortable with negotiation, you're better able to think outside of the box and to be creative with possibilities and solutions. Removing fear and discomfort helps you look at all sides, not just what you have to offer, but also what your potential partner has to offer as well.

Successful negotiation happens when you know exactly what is important and what you can live without. For example, if you're negotiating with a vendor and payment terms are more important to you than price, you can wiggle on the price in exchange for being able to pay on terms that optimize your cash flow. If you're uncomfortable negotiating, it is easy to lose focus on what is truly important to you and your business.

> *"To be successful, you have to be able to relate to people; they have to be satisfied with your personality to be able to do business with you and to build a relationship with mutual trust."*
>
> *- George Ross*

How to be Comfortable Negotiating

View the situation as an opportunity to collaborate. When you view the other person as a partner, it is easier to find a mutually beneficial solution rather than pitting yourself against them. Additionally, if you're going to be doing business with a person or a company then a relationship will develop. How it develops begins right here with your first negotiation. If you approach it as a partnership, you'll both walk away happier.

Know what you want. Decide in advance what you want to walk away, with and try to determine what the other party wants to walk away with. It is likely that somewhere there can be an overlap or a give and take. For example, if you want to resell a product at a 10% markup, and the company wants you to sell it at a 5% markup, the overlap is that 5%. Where you go from there is up to the both of you. You could negotiate a 2% decrease your price and maintain the 5% markup, thus giving you a markup of 7%. That is a very simple example. However, it serves to demonstrate the next point as well.

Startup Strategy

Be prepared. When you know what the other party is seeking and what possible points of contention are likely to come up, you can be prepared to offer solutions. Additionally, be prepared in case you cannot come to an agreement. You're not going to be able to work with everyone. It happens, and if you're prepared for it, it makes it easier to walk away from the table without any resentment.

Be willing to listen. There may be some points that you were unaware of. If you're able to listen, really listen to the other side, you may be able to come up with a solution that works for both of you. Additionally, if your partner can tell that you're really taking their concerns to heart, they may be more willing to work with you.

How to Improve Your Negotiation Skills

Practice! Remember that old adage, practice makes perfect? Well, your mom was right. Practice negotiating and you'll not only become more comfortable with it, you'll get better. How can you practice negotiating? Consider every communication you're involved in as a mini negotiation. Evaluate what you want to get out of it, what your partner wants to get out of it, and how you'll both come to a mutual agreement. You can even practice negotiating with your children; however, don't go overboard with this or they'll expect that they can negotiate everything. Trust me on this!

Prepare. Knowing in advance what you want and what your partner wants will take you a long way toward a successful outcome. If you don't know what they want, ask them. Communication is the first step to building a long and mutually beneficial relationship. Don't be afraid to ask. That being said, know that if they say they can't settle for less than 50%, they most likely can. They are simply hedging their bets, and if you offer 45% and an incentive, they'll probably take it.

Increase your expectations. You usually get what you expect. If you expect to be taken advantage of, then it'll likely happen. If you expect to succeed, then that too will likely occur. If you expect to walk away with 50% of the profits, ask for 60%.

Personalize the interaction. It isn't you against them. You aren't an entity against an entity. You are two people working toward a common goal.

View yourself and your partner as equals. They're not better than you, and they're not beneath you. You each have something to offer or you wouldn't be meeting. Show respect and ask for it in return.

Always, always go into a negotiation knowing what you want. If you don't know what you want, you won't be able to negotiate skillfully.

> *"If you can't go around it, over it, or through it, you had better negotiate with it."*
> *- Ashleigh Brilliant*

Preparing for a Negotiation

Before each negotiation, take a few minutes to consider the following questions.

Why are you negotiating?

Are you hiring a new employee, contracting to have some work done, buying a product or service, choosing a vendor, partnering with another business owner?

Startup Strategy

What is the reason for the negotiation?

What do you want to walk away with in a perfect world?

What does your partner want to walk away with?

What are possible points of contention or disagreement?

What are potential solutions?

How much time do you have to find a solution?

Can the discussion be tabled or is it time sensitive?

Does your partner have a time table?

Can you use that to your advantage?

What are the absolute minimum and maximum you will accept?

What are your expectations?

Who are you working with?

What is their background?

Personality?

Communication style?

Practice Negotiating

List a small project ($50-$100) on Elance.com, and negotiate all the details. If you don't know what to assign, check some of the previous exercises in Section 2 for ideas.

Section #4: Funding and Getting Your Business Up and Running

> *"I have no use for bodyguards, but I have very specific use for two highly trained certified public accountants."*
> *- Elvis Presley*

Kind of funny to see a quote by Elvis Presley in a business guide, but he hit the nail on the head. If you own and operate a business, as he did, it all begins and ends with money. Having experts by your side is a great asset.

Perhaps you'd prefer a quote from a more businesslike icon. There is no better money-making icon than Warren Buffet who said, "The reaction of weak management to weak operations is often weak accounting."

Why are we talking about accounting when this lesson is about financing your business and getting it up and running?

Financing Your Business, Your First Step

> *"Before you can really start setting financial goals, you need to determine where you stand financially."*
> *- David Bach*

Your first step to getting your business up and running is to determine how much money you really need. To determine this, you will want to consider the following questions, and yes, they all lead back to accounting and the dreaded B-Word…budget.

Startup Strategy

1. How much do you have in startup funding, or "next step" funding?
2. What will your actual costs be? (Educated guess)
3. How are you marketing your business, and can this be a source of funding for you?
4. How much are your marketing expenses?
5. How much does it cost to operate your business?

Operating expenses (Overhead) can include:

- Phone lines
- Web site development
- Website hosting
- Merchant accounts
- Shopping cart or Point of sale software
- Outsourcing expenses
- Accountant fees
- Computer
- Printer/fax/phone
- Desk
- Office supplies

1. What is your profit margin? (How much of each sale is left after the product or service is paid for and overhead is met?)
2. Is your business profitable? If not, when will it be?
3. How will you support yourself during slow times?
4. How much will you owe in taxes? (Sales tax, unemployment compensation taxes, state income tax, and federal income tax)
5. How often will you pay your taxes? (Usually quarterly, but sit down with your accountant to see what is best for your business.)

What are Your Financing Options?

Once you have a budget, what are your financing options? Your options are basically divided into three categories: Equity financing, debit financing, and self funding.

Equity financing is giving up some portion of your company in exchange for funds. An example of this would be to give an investor 5% of your profits or to sell them stock in your company. The most obvious benefit to this kind of funding is you don't have to commit to payment terms and pay a percentage back to a lender - you're not borrowing money. You're taking money in exchange for future profits. The downside is that you have to share your profits and often give up some control of the company. This kind of exchange can be as simple as family or friends "investing money" in exchange for a share of the company or as complicated as going after Angel investors and Venture Capital. VCs and Angels are beyond the scope of this guide, but regardless, make sure your accountant and attorney are involved in ANY transaction where you give up equity (a portion of ownership), even if it's just to family and friends. There are legal as well as financial ramifications to this, and you want to make sure you, your business, and your investors are protected.

Debit financing means you quite simply incur future debt for money now. This type of funding takes the following common forms:

- Personal Loans
- Small Business Loans
- Home Equity Loans
- Credit Card Debt

A survey by the Small Business Administration found that over 80% of the small businesses surveyed used some kind of

Startup Strategy

credit and had outstanding debt on their books. Of those, 55% of small firms had some kind of traditional loan, while 71% obtained credit from non-traditional sources, mainly owners' loans and credit cards.

The most frequently used types of credit were personal and business credit cards, lines of credit, and vehicle loans. Of those, 46% of small firms used personal credit cards, 34% used business credit cards, and 28% used lines of credit.

While it appears as if many businesses are using debit financing to fund their business startup, there is also the personal loan, which is a loan from a friend, associate, or family member. The benefit to this type of loan is that you're borrowing money from someone you know and trust, quite possibly at a lower interest rate. The downside is that your relationship may become stressed.

Remember the negotiation skills we talked about in section #2? Use them to negotiate lending terms that will make everyone involved happy.

What Do You Need for a Small Business Loan?

Before you head down to your local bank or jump online to fill out the necessary forms, know that applying for a small business loan isn't like applying for a credit card. You will have some planning to do and some preparation is required.

Keep in mind that unless you have a track record or you are putting up significant collateral, most banks will be reluctant to talk to you about a business loan. Not because your idea is bad, but because the type of lending they understand is collateral-based. They understand Real Estate they can foreclose on or an automobile they can repossess. They can't do much with a business idea or concept, and it scares them.

Don't pit yourself against the bank, understand their fears and their needs, and work with them. You'll likely have to talk to several funding institutions and refine your package before you actually get the funding if this is the route you choose.

Here's what your bank or lender wants to see:

- Your personal credit history
- A detailed business plan
- A summary of your experience and how it benefits and applies to your business
- A summary of your education and how it benefits and applies to your business
- A financial forecast and complete market research of the business you are starting – this can be included in your business plan
- Financial statements. This too can be included in your business plan

Your personal credit history, education, and experience are fairly straightforward. However, a budget and business plan can be a little more complicated.

Developing Your Business Plan

In order to get funding, you are going to need to create a solid business plan. This is a more formal version than the working business plan discussed in earlier sections.

"A business plan is primarily an organizing tool used to simplify and clarify business goals and strategies, which might otherwise appear complex and intimidating. However, a business plan is also a sales tool. If it cannot convince at least one other person of the value of your business idea, then either your idea is not worth pursing,

Startup Strategy

or your plan needs major rewriting."
  - Peter J. Patsula

Common Components of a Business Plan

1. Describe Your Business

What does your business do? What products or services do you provide? How would you describe it to a stranger on the street? For some, this is an easy answer, "I sell children's toys." For others, it is a bit more difficult. Work on your business description until it resembles an "elevator pitch." An elevator pitch is a quick and catchy summary of your business usually designed to sell. In this case, you're selling your ability to pay back a loan by establishing the potential profitability of your business. This section should also include the name and location of your business.

2. Employee/Management Plan

When many people start out in business, they're a one-person operation. That's perfectly acceptable. Write down exactly what your job responsibilities will be. Once you've reached a certain level of success, it may make sense to hire someone to handle the tasks that you either don't like or aren't as skilled in, so that you can focus on your strengths. If you already have employees, then you'll want to include their job descriptions here as well as any unique skills and education they bring to the operation.   You also need to capture who the principal owners of the business will be.

3. Legal Considerations

Here you will answer the following questions:

- What legal structure will you have for your business? Sole proprietorship, partnership, corporation, or Limited Liability Company?
- What type of business licenses do you need to legally operate your business?
- What are your insurance needs? Include insurance on physical buildings, errors and omissions insurance for consulting and coaching businesses, liability, homeowners, and health.
- How will you keep a record of your expenses for tax reporting?

4. Products/Services

Here is where you detail your products or services. What are you selling or providing and what does it cost? What is your business model? For example, if you are opening a business as a bookkeeper, then how will you charge? How will you receive payment? Will you offer multiple services like bookkeeping, payroll services, and collections?

5. Operations

How is your business going to function? Do you need a computer? A website? What will your hours of operation be? What are your financial goals? What are your expenses? List each aspect of your business operations, goals, and needs, and then go into as much detail as possible.

6. Sales and Marketing

Start this section by detailing your target market. Next, describe how you plan on reaching this person and selling your products or services. There are many options here and tons of information about marketing tools you can use right here on the Internet Based Moms website. You may also want to detail how much of your time you plan on spending on marketing related tasks each day, week, or month. Another important aspect of this section is defining your customer and outlining why they want what you will be providing.

7.   Budget

How much money are you starting with? What do you need to buy? A detailed budget is essential for success in obtaining a small business loan.

8.   Financial Statements

How has your company performed to date? If you do not have any financial statements as of yet, including profit and loss statements, then draft a predicted earnings statement, and include your budget with a detailed list of expenses.

Some people prefer to work on paper when they're creating their business plan. Other people prefer to work with a software program or to create their business plan and store it online. If you're looking for a software program, we recommend Business Plan Pro. Business Plan Pro walks you through your business plan step-by-step, and it has a financial planning tool that will make it easy for you and potential investors to analyze the business.

However you create your business plan, it is important to keep it in a place and format that is easily accessible. Remember from Section 1, you're going to be putting on your CEO hat regularly, and being able to access your business plan will make life easier and more productive.

Self-Funding

Not every business needs to seek outside funding, and not every business owner wants to. Self-funding is a very real option for the majority of businesses. Self-funding isn't pulling money you've saved out of your IRA to fund your business. It is more like fund raising for your business.

For example, a business owner who wants to publish a book but doesn't have the funds to pay for the publication expenses can approach a business or two that are relevant to the book and offer them a discounted bulk order in exchange for referencing their business in the book. If you wrote a book on how to house train your dog, you could visit local pet stores and make them an offer. The business wins because they are getting free advertising in your book, and they're able to resell your book in their stores. You win because they've given you the money you need to publish your book.

Self-funding isn't restricted to small business owners. Here's a larger scale example, one of the companies we are working with requires half a million dollars in startup capital. Rather than going to investors, or the bank, they are pre-selling an exclusive package to 24 different clients for $25,000 a piece. That will raise the $500,000 necessary with a $100,000 buffer and the business will maintain control without incurring debt.

Can You Afford to Start Your Business?

The goal of this exercise is to help you determine if you can afford to live off of or rely on your business. Use your notebook to capture the following information

Startup Strategy

What is your net worth (savings, property, and investments minus all debts)?

How much income do you need to make monthly for you and your family to maintain your current standard of living?

Do you have any anticipated major expense in the next 10 years? (For example, buying a house or paying for your children's college tuition.)

How much do you have in savings that can be used to start your new business?

How much do you need to start your business?

How much of your business's financing and other debts will you personally guarantee? Many lenders want to know that you're personally contributing to the startup costs and how much you're contributing.

Do you have any collateral for a loan? If yes, what is it?

Where will you get the rest of the money you need to start your business? (List sources and amounts.)

Other factors to consider:

If necessary, how much credit will you be able to get from suppliers (people you will have to buy goods or services from)?

How much money do you expect to make per year from this business?

Have you already discussed business loans with a banker or an accountant?

Have you considered a partner to supply money or business experience? If yes, who?

Have you investigated the pros and cons of the different entity structures?

Have you discussed your plans with a lawyer?

Are other businesses like the one you want to start doing well in your area?

Are other businesses like the one you want to start doing well in the rest of the country?

Where will you find employees or contractors if you need them?

Will you accept credit cards?

Have you investigated the requirements of credit card companies and the benefits and drawbacks of accepting credit cards?

> *"The entrepreneur is essentially a visualizer and actualizer... He can visualize something, and when he visualizes it he sees exactly how to make it happen."*
> - Robert L. Schwartz

What's Your Business Strategy "Now"?

Earlier in this guide, you did an exercise to evaluate your business strategy. Having read through the guide and completed the other exercises, it is a good idea to spend a little more time fleshing that section out so you can finalize your starting business strategy.

Startup Strategy

You can either use the pages in your notebook that were started in the earlier exercise which should be labeled "STRATEGY" at the top of a page or start fresh. Set aside some time and dive deep into answering the questions from the position of how you want things to be done in your business if it is different than how they are done right now. If you haven't started your business yet, write down how you THINK things will be.

What is your business? Define it.

Who are your customers and what do they need/want? (Age, demographics)

How do you reach your customers? Via internet, bricks and mortar location, the mail, phone or fax, making house calls? Or do you reach them with some combination thereof?

How do you advertise and market to your customers?

How do you differentiate yourself from your competition?

What strengths do you have that make you and your business standout?

What weaknesses do you have and how can you overcome them? For example, low startup financing may be a weakness and a small business loan may be your solution.

How do you charge your customers?

Why are you in business? What are your goals?

What is your exit strategy? How and when do you plan to eventually leave the business?

Inspired Action

Here's where we pull it all together and put it into action. This is the feel-good moment of the guide. True, you already feel good about what you've accomplished, but here is where you plan for the future based on what you've just accomplished.

Take some time, just a bit, and create inspired-action SMART Plans in your notebook. Taking one look back at all you've accomplished will give you a great feeling and show you exactly how much progress you've made.

Go back through your notebook, and list all of your targets, goals, and action steps:

- What steps are you going to take to develop a comprehensive strategy? What tools will you use?
- How are you going to approach funding your next business expansion?
- How are you going to hone your negotiating and deal-making skills?
- How are you going to ensure you're spending time working "ON" your business rather than "IN" it all the time?
- What systems do you need to put into place to make your business work for you?

List one item per line, and after you have them all listed, rank each one in order of priority. Rank the one that will make the biggest impact in your business and your life RIGHT NOW as number 1, the second as number 2 and so on down the list.

Take the top three and create a SMART Plan for each one. Work those plans until you hit the target, then come back,

Startup Strategy

and create SMART Plans for the next three. Remember, a SMART plan must be:

S – pecific

M – easurable

A – ttainable

R – ealistic

T – ime Trackable

Ric Thompson

What's Your Strategy Score NOW?

When you've completed this evaluation, compare the score to the first time you took it. You may be surprised how much you've changed in the short time it's taken you to complete the guide.

On a scale of 1-10 (10 being the highest), rank where you stand now with regard to your business strategy.

I understand the roles of the Technician, the Manager, and the Entrepreneur, and how they apply to my business.

1   2   3   4   5   6   7   8   9   10

I have written long and short term goals as well as a 5-10 year vision for my business.

1   2   3   4   5   6   7   8   9   10

I have a clear picture of my strengths and those of my business, and the competitive advantage that gives us.

1   2   3   4   5   6   7   8   9   10

I have a clear picture of my weaknesses and those of my business, and how to compensate for that.

1   2   3   4   5   6   7   8   9   10

Startup Strategy

I have a clear picture of my opportunities and those of my business, and how to capitalize on them.

1   2   3   4   5   6   7   8   9   10

I have a clear picture of my threats and those of my business, and how to minimize them.

1   2   3   4   5   6   7   8   9   10

I have a defined business model and a structure for how my clients will go through it.

1   2   3   4   5   6   7   8   9   10

I know how my top three competitors do business and how I am differentiating myself.

1   2   3   4   5   6   7   8   9   10

I know exactly who my clients are and what they want

1   2   3   4   5   6   7   8   9   10

I understand the process of a negotiation and all the questions I need to know the answers to before I go into a negotiation

1   2   3   4   5   6   7   8   9   10

I have a good understanding of the funding sources available to my business for startup or expansion

SCORING

Add up all the numbers you circled._____

Divide the total number by 10

Record your NEW "Strategy Score" here _____

Did you see an improvement in your score? Why do you think you did or did not?

Come back in a month, six months, or even a year, and retake the assessment to see how your knowledge and use of your business strategy has changed your business outcomes.

Conclusion

Congratulations on deciding to don your CEO hat and work ON your business rather than only working IN your business! Taking these critical steps will help you guarantee that your business is as strong and profitable as possible! Being an entrepreneur isn't easy, but by taking these steps and developing a sound business strategy, you're ensuring a stronger business and a better life for you and your family.

> *"Working for someone else is nothing like being an entrepreneur and the boss of your own business. To become an entrepreneur requires a different plan or map. You'll be taking a different road, to a different destination."*
>
> *- Noel Peebles, Author of Sell Your Business the Easy Way*

When you have all of these factors accounted for, then and only then can you plan to be in that winning percentage of businesses that are still around and thriving five years from now.

This book provided you with valuable insights into why having a business strategy is crucial to your success, how to develop a business plan used for funding, and how to use your strategy to drive business success. You learned:

- What a business strategy is, and why it is important
- The difference between working ON your business and working IN it
- Why you need to set aside time to wear your CEO hat
- The different business models you can select from
- How to determine competitive advantage
- Tips for negotiating
- The common components of a business plan

- What kind of financing options are available for small businesses

Now it's time to take what you have learned and make a difference in your business. Remember, innovation is the key to the future, embrace it!

Ric Thompson

Check out some of Ric's other books!!

http://www.amazon.com/dp/B00I3Q2QPK

http://www.amazon.com/dp/B00LIGKRCG

Ric Thompson

http://www.amazon.com/dp/B00H4HHY56

http://www.amazon.com/dp/B00L9K6928

www.ingramcontent.com/pod-product-compliance
Lightning Source LLC
Chambersburg PA
CBHW071812170526
45167CB00003B/1277